WHEN I'M GONE

The Ultimate Practical End-of-Life Planner

ASHA
— PRESS —

This planner is part of the Practical End-of-Life Planning set of books by Green Sauce Publishing. The content of this book, including its structure, text, and layout, is protected under international copyright law.

While the interiors of all books in this series share the same content, each edition is uniquely presented with its own distinct cover design to provide a range of options for users.

For permissions or inquiries, please visit:
https://www.greensaucepublishing.com.
Published by Green Sauce Publishing.

"For life and death are one, even as the river and the sea are one."

— Kahlil Gibran

Table of Contents

Who is this book for?

This planner has been designed to provide you with a structured, organized space for documenting your essential information, together with your wishes and preferences for the end of your life. By doing so, you can relieve your loved ones of the burden of making difficult decisions during a time of grief and ensure that your final wishes are known and can be respected.

Whether you have purchased this planner for yourself, or as a gift for someone else, or you have received it as a gift from a loved one, it can serve multiple purposes:

For Older Adults: When entering your senior years, it is natural to reflect on your life and consider your legacy. This planner helps you document your wishes regarding your healthcare, finances, and personal legacy, providing a sense of control and peace of mind.

For Younger People Facing a life-limiting condition: Life is unpredictable, and sometimes we are faced with challenges that lead us to confront our mortality sooner than expected. Whether due to illness, accidents, or other circumstances, this planner allows you to make your voice heard and your wishes known, even in the face of uncertainty.

For Anyone Preparing for the Unexpected: Accidents and sudden illnesses can happen to anyone, at any age. Having a well-organized end-of-life plan ensures that your loved ones are not left with unanswered questions or difficult decisions. This planner is a tool for anyone who wants to be prepared, no matter what the future holds.

Introduction

Note this book is NOT a Will, a legal document or a binding contract or agreement. Your Will should be made and kept separately, with the location recorded in this book.

We suggest you attach a couple of strong 8″ x 10″ envelopes inside the covers of this book. You can use them to store receipts, copies of important documents or anything else you would like to keep with your planner. You could add your passport and citizenship papers and other hard-to-replace documents to the envelopes - and then place this planner in a safe and secure location where you can easily and quickly grab it in case of fire or other emergency.

Fill out each section as it is relevant to you. If a section is not relevant to you, leave it blank, or use it to record other information particular to you. Where you know information may change we suggest using pencil. There are additional pages at the end of each Section, and at the back of the book, in case you run out of space. Another option is to save frequently changing information on a separate sheet in one of the envelopes and replace it at intervals.

Take your time to reflect, then fill each section out as you feel ready. This is a deeply personal process. There is no right or wrong way to approach it. The most important thing is that it reflects your true wishes and provides clarity for those you leave behind. It is also important to consider your preferences in the event that you may find yourself in unexpected circumstances where you remain alive but are unable to communicate your wishes to your family.

Very Important: Store this book in a safe, secure place each time you have finished using it - and let only your closest family, legal representative or Executor know of the location.

While this planner is a tool for you, it also represents a profound act of love for your family and friends. By preparing in advance, you give your loved ones the comfort of knowing they are honoring your wishes, and preventing unexpected expense or awkward surprises for them in their time of grief. During a period of bereavement, this can bring immeasurable solace.Thinking about the end of our lives can be uncomfortable, but by addressing it with compassion and intention, we can live our remaining days knowing we've provided clarity and peace for those we leave behind. This planner is your gentle guide on that journey.

Personal Information

About Me

Full Legal Name	
Alternative Name/s	
Date and Place of Birth	
Marital Status	
Father's Legal Name	
Mother's Legal Name	
Next of Kin/ Power of Attorney	
Spouse's Legal Name	
Date of Marriage	
Spouse Contact (if Different)	
Occupation and Employer	
Employer's Contact	

More About Me

Emergency Contacts	
Religion Contacts	
Cultural Affiliations	
Social Club Memberships & Contacts	

Children

Name	Date of Birth and Contact Details

Grandchildren

Name	Date of Birth and Contact Details

Grandchildren

Name	Date of Birth and Contact Details

Siblings

Name	Date of Birth and Contact Details

Siblings

Name	Date of Birth and Contact Details

Other Family Contacts

Name	Date of Birth and Contact Details

Other Family Contacts

Name	Date of Birth and Contact Details

Close Friends

Name	Date of Birth and Contact Details

Close Friends

Name	Date of Birth and Contact Details

Business Contacts

Name	Date of Birth and Contact Details

Business Contacts

Name	Date of Birth and Contact Details

Business Contacts

Name	Date of Birth and Contact Details

Personal Contacts

Name	Date of Birth and Contact Details

Personal Contacts

Name	Date of Birth and Contact Details

Personal Contacts

Name	Date of Birth and Contact Details

My Pets

Name	
Date of Birth	
Type of Animal	
Vet Name and Contact	
Nominated Carer	
Name	
Date of Birth	
Type of Animal	
Vet Name and Contact	
Nominated Carer	
Name	
Date of Birth	
Type of Animal	
Vet Name and Contact	
Nominated Carer	

My Pets

Name	
Date of Birth	
Type of Animal	
Vet Name and Contact	
Nominated Carer	
Name	
Date of Birth	
Type of Animal	
Vet Name and Contact	
Nominated Carer	
Name	
Date of Birth	
Type of Animal	
Vet Name and Contact	
Nominated Carer	

Notes

Notes

Notes

Notes

Legal and Financial Matters

Power of Attorney

Name	
Contact Details	
Location of Relevant Documents	

Will

Original Last Will and Testament Location	
Copies of Last Will and Testament Location/s	
Additional Beneficiaries not listed elsewhere	

Will Information

<table>
<tr><td rowspan="5">Estate Planner's Contact Details</td><td></td></tr>
<tr><td></td></tr>
<tr><td></td></tr>
<tr><td></td></tr>
<tr><td></td></tr>
<tr><td rowspan="7">Executors' Contact Details</td><td></td></tr>
<tr><td></td></tr>
<tr><td></td></tr>
<tr><td></td></tr>
<tr><td></td></tr>
<tr><td></td></tr>
<tr><td></td></tr>
</table>

Legal Representatives

Legal Representative Responsibilities and Contact Details	
Legal Representative Responsibilities and Contact Details	

Legal Documents

Document	Location

Insurance Policies

Type of Insurance	Insurance Company	Policy Number	Renewal Date

Money

Accountant			
Bookkeeper			
Bank	Account Type	Account Name	Account Number
Safety Deposit Box Location and Access			

Credit & Store Cards

Card Type	Account Name	Account Number

Mortgages & Loans

Type of Loan	Account Details	Finance Company

Online Banking

Bank	Account Details	Login Details or their Location

Stockmarket & Crypto

Name	Location	Login Details or their Location

Asset Management

Asset Type	Details	How it is Managed

Property Management

Property Manager	Contact Details	Assets Managed

Joint Assets

Partner Names	Contact Details	Type and Percentage of Assets Managed

Bills to Pay

Regular Big Bills to Pay	Amount/s and from Which Account

Bills to Pay

Regular Big Bills to Pay	Amount/s and from Which Account

Cancel Subscriptions

Subscription	Contact/Login and Due Dates

Cancel Subscriptions

Subscription	Contact/Login and Due Dates

Notes

Notes

Digital Footprint

Phones & Passwords

Cell Phone Access Passwords	Subscription/Plan Details

Computers & Passwords

Computers	Access Codes and WiFi Passwords
Location of Dated Password List	
Repair Services Used	
Other Important Information	

Digital Services

Domain and Hosting Services	Account Details

Digital Subscriptions

Subscription Services	Account Details

Social Media

Platform	Account Details and Passwords

Email Accounts

Name	Account Details

My Websites

URL	Hosting Account Details

My Domain Names

Domain Names	Domain Provider Account Details

Digital File Storage

Storage Name	Account Details and what is stored

Notes

Notes

Healthcare: Directives and Preferences

Healthcare Providers

Name	Specialty	Contact Details

Medical History

Medical History

Allergies

Vaccination Records

Current Medication

Date	Medication	Prescribed By

Current Medication

Date	Medication	Prescribed By

Current Medication

Date	Medication	Prescribed By

Prescription Repeats

Date	Medication	Location of Pharmacy

Prescription Repeats

Date	Medication	Location of Pharmacy

Allied Health

Rehab, Physio OT, etc	Provider, Contact and Account Details

Advance Directives

Date	Directive	Location

Medical Wishes

Organ Donation

Notes

Notes

Final Arrangements

My Final Wishes

My Final Wishes

My Final Wishes

My Final Wishes

My Final Wishes

Notes and Messages

Notes and Messages

Notes and Messages

Additional Notes

Notes

Notes

Notes

Notes

Notes

We'd Love to Hear From You

Thank you for choosing **When I'm Gone: The Ultimate Practical End-of-Life Planner.** We hope this planner has helped you take care of the details that matter, giving you peace of mind and making things easier for the people you care about.

If you found this planner helpful, we'd truly appreciate it if you could take a moment to leave a review where you purchased the book. Your feedback helps others decide if this book is right for them—and it helps us continue creating practical, no-nonsense tools that make a real difference.

Additionally, you can the **QR code** to visit our website, where you can:

- Leave a review
- Explore our other practical life planners and journals
- Sign up for updates and new releases from Asha Press

We'd also love to connect with you on social media. Share your thoughts, experiences, or ideas using the hashtag **#WhenImGonePlanne**r and tag **@AshaPress.**

Let's keep the conversation going—because planning ahead is one of the kindest things we can do.

ASHA
— PRESS —

The Asha Press Team

Made in United States
North Haven, CT
05 November 2026

21767746R00054